THIS BOOK BELONGS TO

RISE AND SHINE

"YOU ARE THE LIGHT OF THE WORLD...LET YOUR LIGHT SHINE..."

~ MATTHEW 5: 14-16

"HONOR YOUR FATHER AND MOTHER."
~ EXODUS 20:12

WHY SHOULD I HONOR MY FATHER AND MOTHER?

_____

_____

_____

"I PRAISE YOU BECAUSE I AM FEARFULLY AND WONDERFULLY MADE."

~ PSALMS 139:14

I PRAISE GOD BECAUSE...

_____

_____

_____

_____

_____

_____

"YOU ARE THE LIGHT
OF THE WORLD."

~ MATTHEW 5:14

"MAN SHALL NOT LIVE ON BREAD ALONE BUT ON EVERY WORD THAT COMES FROM THE MOUTH OF GOD."

~ MATTHEW 4:4

I AM A LIGHT IN THE WORLD

DRAW A SHINING SUN.

WHY IS BREAKFAST THE MOST IMPORTANT MEAL OF THE DAY?

FILL IN THE BLANKS:

_____

_____

_____

_____

_____

_____

_____

_____

_____

_____

"SHE DRESSES HERSELF WITH STRENGTH AND MAKES HER ARMS STRONG." ~

PROVERBS 31:17

AND

"A WISE MAN IS FULL OF STRENGTH, AND A MAN OF KNOWLEDGE ENHANCES HIS MIGHT." ~ PROVERBS 24:5

HOW CAN I MAKE MY BODY AND SPIRIT STRONG?

_____

_____

_____

_____

"BLESSED ARE THE GENTLE FOR THEY SHALL INHERIT THE EARTH."
~ MATTHEW 5:5

HOW CAN I BE MORE GENTLE WITH MY FRIENDS AND FAMILY?

FILL IN THE BLANKS:

_____

_____

_____

_____

CIRCLE THE LINE THAT LEADS TO THE SCHOOL DOOR

WORD SEARCH

"WORDS OF JOY AND INSPIRATION"

JOY

WORDS TO FIND:

JOY
FUTURE
ASK
ROUTINE,
TIME
RISE
SHINE
LIGHT
WORLD
READ

```
J O Y R E A D L T I M E W O R K
L S E H G I S E H R W O R L D D
K C O H I N E T H G I L U R E O
O F U T U R E P A I N T G C A G
C H O R E S G B U T T E R F L Y
R O P R A S K R E E C A E P
I S L E A S H I N E A M L H H
S C S I H W O R K H E L P O O
E E A L O O H C S R G R O W L
S T E A M P L A Y E D C H O O
```

WORDS TO FIND:

PEACE
GROW
WORK
HELP
BUTTERFLY
DOG
CHORES
TEAM
SCHOOL
PAINT
PLAY

"HAVING WISDOM AND UNDERSTANDING IS BETTER THAN HAVING SILVER OR GOLD."
~ PROVERBS 16:16

MATCH

DRAW A LINE FROM EACH PERSON AND OBJECT TO THEIR EXACT MATCH.

"LOVE EACH OTHER AS I HAVE LOVED YOU."

~ JOHN 15:12-13

HOW MANY HEARTS CAN YOU FIND AND CIRCLE ?

_____

"HE HAS FILLED THEM WITH SKILL TO DO ALL KINDS OF WORK AS ENGRAVERS, DESIGNERS, EMBROIDERERS IN BLUE, PURPLE AND SCARLET YARN AND FINE LINEN AND WEAVERS. —ALL OF THEM SKILLED WORKERS AND DESIGNERS."

~ EXODUS 35:35

"FOR YOU ARE THE GOD WHO SEES ME"

THANK YOU, LORD, FOR SEEING ME AND FOR MY TALENTS!

DRAW A PICTURE USING THESE COLORS:

BLUE, PINK, RED, YELLOW AND GREEN

HOW MANY WORDS CAN YOU MAKE USING

THE LETTERS:

GOD SEES ME

UNSCRAMBLE THESE WORDS:

UCSIM _____

EARTCE _____

ROOLC _____

TAR _____

SLEHP _____

WORG _____

DORL _____

SLIKSL _____

LUBE _____

KNIP _____

DER _____

RENGE _____

HINT:

(MUSIC, CREATE, COLOR, ART, HELPS, GROW, LORD, SKILLS, BLUE, PINK, RED, GREEN)

WORD SEARCH

"WORDS OF FAITH AND GRATITUDE"

WORDS TO FIND:

THANKS, HOPE, BLESSED, SEEK, PLANS, LORD, MUSIC, SING, PRAISE, WORSHIP, LOVE, PRAY, GRATEFUL, COLOR, GO, PEACE

```
P R A I S E L H O P E W O R S H I P
L O R D S I N G R S E E K M U S I C
B L E S S E D P A N R E T I R T R O
G R A T E F U L A R P E A C E L V A
H O P R A I S E R O E A R L R S H P
P R O L O R D K E S H E M U S I C R
S P R A Y F L O V E I W O R S H I P
K N S E E K N I S G S I N G L P R A
N P L A N S A M S I S I N G P R A Y
A L O V E L G O E L L E R S E E K H
H E K M U S I C O L O R P L A N S
T P R A I S E P G R A T E F U L H O
```

Grateful and Thankful

"I CAN DO ALL THINGS THROUGH HIM WHO STRENGTHENS ME."
~ 2 PHILLIPIANS 4:13

CIRCLE WHAT IS DIFFERENT IN ONE OF THE PICTURES.

MATCH

"SO GOD MADE THE WILD ANIMALS, THE TAME ANIMALS AND ALL THE SMALL CRAWLING ANIMALS TO PRODUCE MORE OF THEIR OWN KIND."

 ~ GENESIS 1:25-31

DRAW A LINE TO THE EXACT MATCHING DOGS:

"MAY THE FAVOR OF THE LORD OUR GOD BE UPON US,
AND ESTABLISH THE WORK OF OUR HANDS UPON US;
YES, ESTABLISH THE WORK OF OUR HANDS!"
~ PSALMS 90:17

DRAW A PICTURE OF WHAT YOU'D LIKE TO BE WHEN YOU GROW UP:

"SING TO GOD, SING PRAISES TO HIS NAME;

LIFT UP A SONG TO HIM WHO RIDES THROUGH THE DESERTS;

HIS NAME IS THE LORD; EXULT BEFORE HIM!"

~ PSALMS 68:4-6

CIRCLE ALL OF THE WORDS THAT RHYME

WITH... SONG.

LONG

SUN

FUN

WRONG

SING

STRONG

ALONG

BELONG

" I PRAISE YOU GOD, FOR I AM FEARFULLY AND WONDERFULLY MADE."

~ PSALMS 139:14

"YOU CAN REST WITHOUT WORRY OR FEAR BECAUSE
WHILE YOU REST GOD IS WATCHING OVER YOU."
~ PSALMS 33:8

FILL IN THE BLANKS:

YOU CAN _____ WITHOUT

_____ OR _____ BECAUSE

WHILE YOU _____ GOD IS

_____ OVER YOU."

~ PSALMS __:_

"AN ATHLETE IS NOT CROWNED UNLESS HE COMPETES ACCORDING TO THE RULES."

~ 2 TIMOTHY 2:5

DRAW A CROWN ON EACH OF THE CHARACTERS.

DRAW A LINE TO THE NAME OF EACH BALL.

TENNIS BALL

BASEBALL

BOWLING BALL

BASKETBALL

SOCCER BALL

"GUIDE ME IN YOUR TRUTH AND TEACH ME, FOR YOU ARE GOD MY SAVIOR, AND MY HOPE IS IN YOU ALL THE DAYS LONG."

~ PSALMS 25:5

DRAW A LINE CONNECTING ALL OF THE BUTTERFLIES IN THE PICTURE BELOW.

HOW MANY BUTTERFLIES ARE BELOW?

_____

FILL IN THE BLANKS:

GUIDE ME IN YOUR _ _ _ _ _
AND _ _ _ _ _ _ ME,
FOR YOU ARE MY _ _ _ _ _ _,
AND MY _ _ _ _ _, IS IN _ _ _ ALL _ _ _
_ _ _ _ LONG.

~ PSALM _ _:_

UNSCRAMBLE THESE WORDS:

RONGTS   _ _ _ _ _ _

THERA   _ _ _ _ _

EPOH   _ _ _ _

DORL   _ _ _ _

VIGDE   _ _ _ _ _

THURT   _ _ _ _ _

EACHT   _ _ _ _ _

HINT:

(STRONG, HEART, HOPE, LORD, GUIDE, TRUTH, TEACH)

HOW MANY HORSES DO YOU SEE? CIRCLE THEM.

_____

"JESUS DECLARED, I AM THE BREAD OF LIFE. WHOMEVER COMES TO ME WILL NEVER GO HUNGRY AND WHOMEVER BELIEVES IN ME WILL NEVER BE THIRSTY."

~ JOHN 6:35

HOW MANY LOAVES OF BREAD DO YOU COUNT?

_____

HOW MANY FISHES DO YOU COUNT?

_____

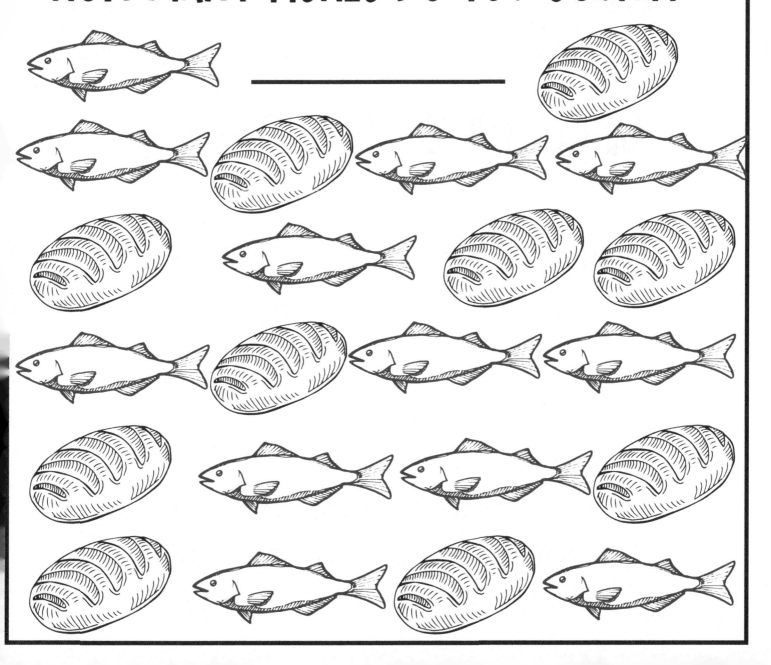

"HOW GOOD AND PLEASANT IT IS WHEN GOD'S PEOPLE LIVE TOGETHER IN UNITY." ~ PSLAMS 133:1

WHY IS EATING TOGETHER IMPORTANT QUALITY TIME?

CIRCLE THE CORRECT ANSWERS:

A) TALK AND TELL STORIES ~ B) WE SPEND TIME TOGETHER

C) WE FORM GOOD EATING HABITS AND A ROUTINE

D) IT FEELS GOOD ~ E) IT FEELS BAD

F) IT'S TIME TO PLAY WITH MY TABLET

G) IT CAN HELP ME GET BETTER GRADES

H) IT HELPS ME BEHAVE BETTER

I) WE MAKE GOOD MEMORIES ~ J) IT IS NOT QUALITY TIME

EATING TOGETHER IS IMPORTANT QUALITY TIME!

NO TELEVISION, NO TABLETS, NO CELL PHONES, NO BOOKS,
NO DISTRACTIONS. IT'S A TIME TO TALK, SHARE STORIES ABOUT OUR DAY
AND ENJOY TIME WITH EACH OTHER.

WORD SEARCH

"DAILY ROUTINES AND WELLNESS"

WORDS TO FIND:

BREAKFAST, PLAY, REST, DINNER, THINK, FRUIT, ICE CREAM, FOCUS, CLEAN, HEALTH, EXERCISE

```
THINKRESTFOCUSPLAY
REAKFREAKFASTDINNE
ICECREAMCHEALTHINC
CLEANBREAKFASTFURE
ELINNERHEALTHEAKPR
CREAMPLAYEAREKFRUI
RESTBREAKFASTREACL
EXERCISEHITICECREA
AKFRUITHEALTHPLAYE
MRESTFOCUSBREAKFAS
HPLAYDINNERHEALTHE
```

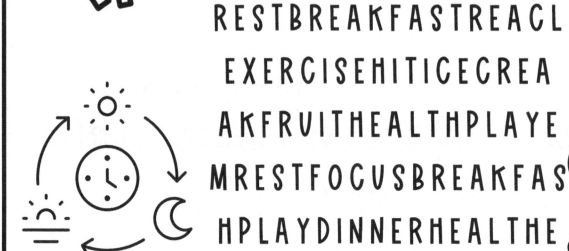

"HOW SWEET ARE YOUR WORDS TO MY TASTE,
SWEETER THAN HONEY TO MY MOUTH." ~ PSLAMS 119:103

1) HOW MANY ICE CREAM CONES ARE THERE? _____

2) HOW MANY ICE CREAM BOWLS ARE THERE? _____

3) HOW MANY ICE CREAM SCOOPS TOTAL ARE THERE?_____

4) DRAW A CIRCLE AROUND ALL THE ICE CREAM CONES.

5) DRAW A SQUARE AROUND ALL THE ICE CREAM BOWLS.

"PRAISE HIM WITH TRUMPET SOUND; PRAISE HIM WITH LUTE AND HARP! PRAISE HIM WITH TAMBOURINE AND DANCE; PRAISE HIM WITH STRINGS AND PIPE! PRAISE HIM WITH SOUNDING CYMBALS; PRAISE HIM WITH LOUD CLASHING CYMBALS!." ~ PSLAMS 150:1-6

HOW MANY MUSICAL NOTES DO YOU SEE?

_____

FOR EACH MUSICAL NOTE WRITE A WORD

FROM THE VERSE,

~ PSALMS 150:1-6

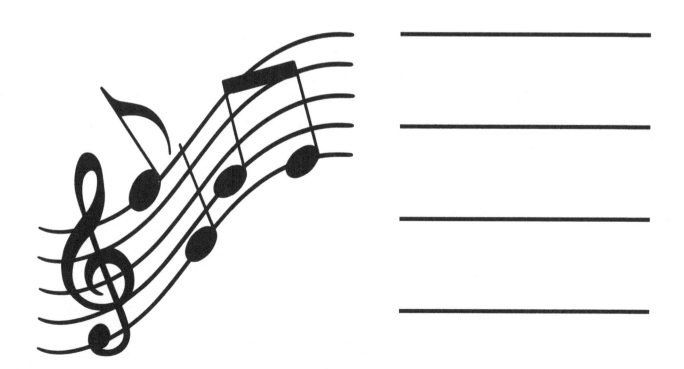

_____

_____

_____

_____

"CHILDREN OBEY YOUR PARENTS IN EVERYTHING, FOR THIS PLEASES THE LORD."
~ COLOSSIANS 3:20

DRAW A LINE FROM EVERY TOY INTO THE TOY CHEST.

ALL HARD WORK BRINGS A PROFIT.
~PROVERBS 14:23

FILL IN THE BLANKS:

ALL HARD ____ BRINGS

A _____.

CHILDREN ____ YOUR _____

IN _____, FOR THIS

_____ THE ____.

1) CIRCLE THE GIFT THAT IS TRULY DIFFERENT.

2) WHAT MAKES THIS GIFT SPECIAL?

CIRCLE ONE ANSWER:

A) CHILDREN ARE A GIFT FROM GOD

B) IT'S WRAPPED SO PRETTY

THERE IS ONLY ONE OF YOU IN THIS WHOLE ENTIRE WORLD!

EACH CHILD AND PERSON IS A GIFT FROM GOD AND EVERYONE IS UNIQUE.

CIRCLE ALL THAT HAS BREATH
TO PRAISE THE LORD.

"CREATE IN ME A CLEAN HEART, OH GOD,
AND RENEW A RIGHT SPIRIT WITHIN ME." ~ PSALMS 51:10

HOW MANY FISHES DO YOU COUNT?

_____

CIRCLE THEM.

 # RHYMING WORDS

DRAW A LINE CONNECTING THE WORDS THAT RHYME:

CLEAN	SMART
BATH	TROUBLES
BUBBLES	PATH
FISH	WISH
SOAP	BEAN
HEART	TRUE
RENEW	HOPE

"GOD DIDN'T GIVE US A SPIRIT THAT MAKES US WEAK AND FEARFUL. HE GAVE US A SPIRIT THAT GIVES US POWER AND LOVE. IT HELPS US CONTROL OURSELVES.

~ 2 TIMOTHY 1:7

WHICH DAY DID GOD REST?

CIRCLE ONE ANSWER.

A) THE FIRST DAY

B) THE 7TH DAY KNOWN AS SABBATH

CIRCLE ALL OF THE SUNDAYS ON THE CALENDAR.

DAYS OF THE WEEK:

FILL IN THE BLANKS & TRACE THE NUMBERS:

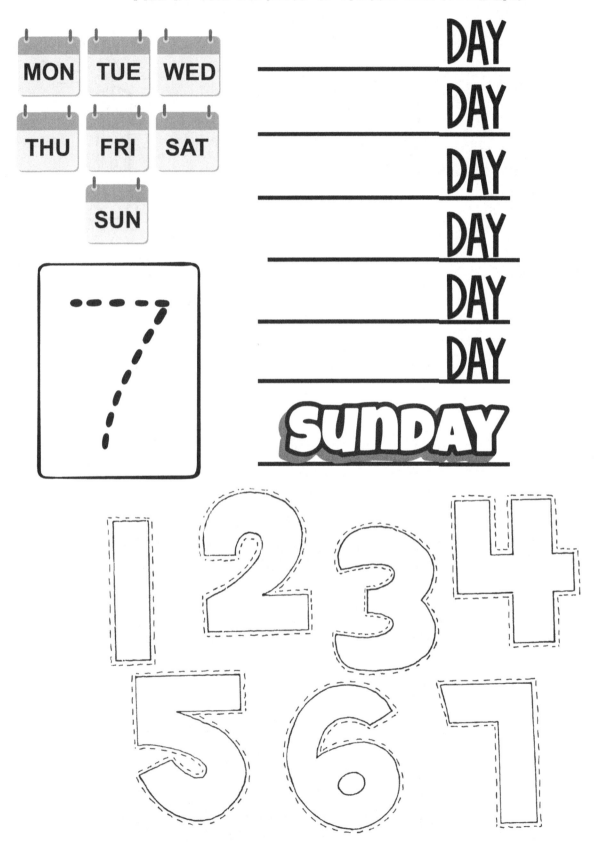

MON TUE WED
THU FRI SAT
SUN

7

_____ DAY
_____ DAY
_____ DAY
_____ DAY
_____ DAY
_____ DAY
_____ SUNDAY

1 2 3 4
5 6 7

HOW MANY WORDS CAN YOU MAKE USING THE LETTERS IN: JESUS CHRIST

_____

_____

_____

_____

_____

_____

_____

_____

_____

_____

"GIVE THANKS TO THE LORD,
FOR HE IS GOOD.
HIS LOVE
ENDURES FOREVER."

~ PSALMS 136:1

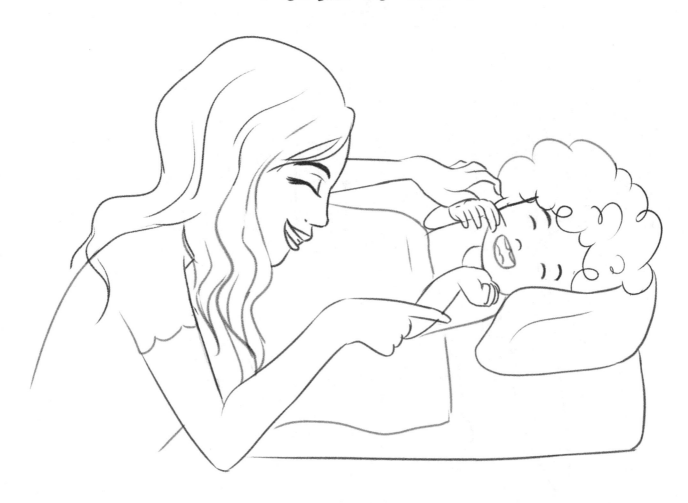

FILL IN THE BLANKS:

GIVE _____ TO THE ____, FOR HE IS ____.

HIS ____ ENDURES _____.

PSALMS ___:_

I AM THANKFUL FOR:

WORD SEARCH

JESUS SAYS I AM:

CALLED, CHOSEN, LOVED, FORGIVEN, CLEAN,
CHILD, HOLY, WONDERFUL, STRONG, NEW.

FIND AND CIRCLE THE WORDS LISTED ABOVE:

```
C H O S E N  A G L O V E D E
L G N O R T S D N E R  H C C
E M  F O R G I V E N A D W H
A B M W C A L L E D E R  E I
N E W W O N D E R F U L N L
E D I H O L Y C  LE  A  N D
```

THE WORDS CAN BE FOUND HORIZONTALLY, VERTICALLY, OR DIAGONALLY,
AND THEY MAY BE WRITTEN FORWARDS OR BACKWARD.
ENJOY SOLVING THE PUZZLE!

TIME TO RHYME!

TRACE THE WORD ON THE LEFT AND THEN DRAW A LINE
TO THE WORD ON THE RIGHT THAT RHYMES WITH IT.

PRAY	DRESSED
LOVE	GROW
TEAM	SAY
SOW	DREAM
BLESSED	DOVE

BELIEVE IN THE LORD,
JESUS CHRIST, AND YOU WILL BE SAVED.
~ ACTS 16:31

COLOR BY NUMBER

1.GREEN 2. BROWN 3. YELLOW 4. BLUE 5. ORANGE 6. BLACK 7. GREY 8. RED
9. PURPLE 10. LAVENDER

"PRAY WITHOUT CEASING."

~ I THESOLONNIANS 5:17